A SENSE OF DIRECTION

The Basic Elements of th
Spiritual Journey

GW01003776

Louis J. Cameli
Robert L. Miller
Gerard P. Weber

TABOR
PUBLISHING

Valencia, California   Allen, Texas

Send all inquiries to:
Tabor Publishing
25115 Avenue Stanford, Suite 130
Valencia, California 91355

Printed in the United States of America

ISBN 0-89505-447-7

1 2 3 4 5   90 89 88 87

CONTENTS

INTRODUCTION

In an age of quick fixes and how-to books on every subject, a book on the basic elements of the spiritual journey is not likely to be popular, for this journey does not lend itself to quick fixes and simple how-to techniques. Deep and lasting relationships with God and neighbor do not come easily.

This book is an attempt to distill the wisdom of the tradition of Christian spirituality into a few basic principles for those who embark on the journey. It is intended for those who have felt the call of God to a closer union with God and who wish to move ahead on this journey. It is a book not merely to read but to reflect upon and discuss with a spiritual friend, a spiritual director, or a group of people seeking to grow spiritually.

This book is not the work of a great spiritual master or guru. It is the result of the combined efforts of three ordinary priests deeply interested in helping people along the journey. Each has contributed his own experience and expertise to the project. Father Louis Cameli, professor of spirituality and spiritual director at Mundelein Seminary of the University of St. Mary of the Lake, Mundelein, Illinois, has his doctorate in spiritual theology. Father Robert Miller is a pastor in Rialto, California, and has worked very successfully with groups interested in growing spiritually. Father Gerard Weber was a parish priest for thirty years and for the past thirteen years has produced programs of religious growth for adults.

The principles of spiritual growth outlined in this book are simple:

1. Our deepest need and hunger is for God, and we become more aware of this as we reflect about life.
2. The spiritual life is a journey toward the God who is love, a process of deepening our relationships with God and with one another.
3. On this journey, God speaks to us through the Scriptures.
4. On this journey, we need to reach out to God in prayer.
5. Our spiritual journey takes place in the context of the Church, made up of Christian fellow travelers.
6. The journey involves struggle with obstacles both within us and outside us.
7. We need discipline, conscious patterns of living, as we make the journey.

8. We need discernment to make the choices that will keep us on the path that is best for us.

Each chapter explores the meaning of one of these principles. Interspersed throughout each chapter are questions to help readers reflect on how they have already practiced and experienced the principle in their lives. There are no right or wrong answers to these questions. They are intended to help readers surface their ideas and feelings about the material in the chapter. An individual may use them for his or her own reflection, or a group may use them to stimulate discussion about the topic. It is not necessary to discuss all the questions in each activity. Readers should use those that produce the best insights and discussion. Readers can use the space provided below each question to jot down their ideas or feelings. Each chapter concludes by asking readers what they would like to see happen in their own lives and gives a practice exercise for using this principle in making their own spiritual journey.

The authors make no promises that a person's life will be changed, but they do believe that any lasting progress on the spiritual journey is based on understanding and consciously appreciating the importance of each principle of spiritual growth.

1

WHERE DO WE BEGIN?

"Is there any point to my life?" "Is this all there is?" "How do I get closer to God?" Whoever has asked these or similar questions has really been asking, "How do I grow spiritually?" Questions like these are the starting point for any real spiritual growth and development. Yet many people feel that the word *spiritual* is too lofty or removed from their everyday experience. They think that spirituality deals with something "beyond them," with something reserved for a chosen few.

The Gospels tell us that Jesus invited ordinary people to follow him. Like people today, they were filled with questions about the meaning of their lives and about how they related to God. People today still are struggling with these same questions. Jesus still invites them to follow him and learn from him how to answer their own questions.

The next day John was here again with two of his disciples. As he watched Jesus walk by, he said, "Look! There is the Lamb of God!" The two disciples heard what he said, and followed Jesus. When Jesus turned around and noticed them following him, he asked them, "What are you looking for?"
                                                                    John 1:35–38

- Up to now, what has been your experience in trying to lead a spiritual life?

- What are you looking for from reading this book (or from sharing with this group)?

- What questions about life and your personal relationship with God do you have at present?

7

Stopping to Reflect

Recently, a woman stood at the bedside of her husband in an intensive-care unit as he struggled to breathe after a massive heart attack. She turned to the chaplain and said, "I don't know where all the years have gone. It seemed that they all rushed by, and I didn't even notice." Her husband's heart attack caused her to think about some of the "larger issues" of life.

At times we all hear ourselves echoing her words. We, too, live lives for the most part taking things for granted, constantly moving—sometimes rapidly, sometimes even frantically, but generally not thoughtfully or reflectively. Then a crisis forces us to stop and reflect about the larger issues of life.

- Reflect upon a crisis moment in your own life. What happened?

- What feelings did you experience?

- What questions came to your mind?

- How did you see things differently?

- What changes, if any, did you make in your life?

- What changes in your life at present are urging you to grow spiritually? Be very specific about a change in a relationship, in your health, in your job, in your feelings about yourself or about life.

Our Hungers and God's Offer

If people are to grow spiritually, they must be in touch with the fundamental realities of their lives, with where they are going, and with where they really want to go. Jesus told a story about a man at a crisis moment, a man who was not in touch with the reality of life.

> "There was a rich man who had a good harvest. 'What shall I do?' he asked himself. 'I have no place to store my harvest. I know!' he said. 'I will pull down my grain bins and build larger ones. All my grain and my goods will go there. Then I will say to myself: You have blessings in reserve for years to come. Relax! Eat heartily, drink well. Enjoy yourself.' But God said to him, 'You fool! This very night your life shall be required of you. To whom will all this piled-up wealth of yours go?' That is the way it works with those who grow rich for themselves instead of growing rich in the sight of God."
>
> Luke 12:16–21

Frequent critical reflection is the key to being in touch with the direction of our lives. It prevents us from taking things for granted. We need not only to look at the crises in our lives, but also on a regular basis to stop and look at the small, ordinary, routine events of life. This reflection puts us in touch with our hungers and, if done with faith, opens us to the offer that God makes in Jesus Christ. God's offer is not a solution to human problems but a commitment to be with us as we work through them.

- In the parable, what hunger was the person trying to satisfy?

- Why or why not was the person able to satisfy the need?

- What hungers are you trying to satisfy?

9

- How well do you think your efforts are succeeding?

- How is this parable a challenge from Jesus for you to get in touch with what is really important in life?

- What kinds of things do you see people relying on for a sense of security?

Our Deepest Hunger

To grow spiritually, people need to recognize their deepest hungers. Psychologists tell us that all our psychological hungers or desires can be reduced to four: the desire to love and be loved, the desire to know, the desire to grow, and the desire to live forever. These four desires ultimately can be satisfied only by God. But people do not always recognize and acknowledge that the deepest reality of life is God and that these desires are really a sign of their hunger for God.

The people who flocked around Jesus were hungering for a better life. They were restless, not satisfied with their present life. Among them were tax collectors who were actually collaborating with the occupying Roman army. There were prostitutes, thieves, and any number of unsavory characters, as well as the sick, the lame, and the blind. In fact, Jesus' enemies derided him as "a friend of sinners." The main group of people who did not respond to Jesus were the self-righteous, who were satisfied with themselves and their way of life. These people felt they had earned their place with God; they felt no need for what Jesus had to offer. They stood in judgment of others, but they could not look at themselves.

Many of these hungry, restless, lonely outcasts became disciples of Jesus. They formed a community around him.

Now it happened that, while Jesus was at table in Matthew's home, many tax collectors and those known as sinners came to join Jesus and his disciples at dinner. The Pharisees saw this and complained to his disciples, "What reason can the

Teacher have for eating with tax collectors and those who disregard the law?" Overhearing the remark, he said: "People who are in good health do not need a doctor; sick people do."

Matthew 9:10–12

When people live their lives reflectively, that is, not taking things for granted or living presumptuously, they recognize that their hunger is to be in harmony with God, to be so close to God as to share in God's very life. The goal of human life has been expressed as seeing God face to face, as sharing a life of loving union with God. Words like these make this experience seem static and even unattractive. Yet, even now, we can begin to experience the magnetic power of this union. We can have moments of being lost in something beautiful. At times, we can feel an intense peace in surrendering to the larger mystery of life. And, perhaps most powerful of all, we can experience the thrill and joy of being united with another in full and unconditional acceptance. These experiences are but a mild foretaste of the ways in which the deepest human hunger will be satisfied. They are but fleeting glimpses of the loving union with God that humans are destined to achieve.

Saint Augustine said, "You have created us for yourself, O God. Our hearts are restless until they rest in you." His words are another way of expressing this destiny. We need to know the restlessness, the deep longing, the hunger for God that has been planted in human hearts. Entertainment, work, even relationships can all too often be the means by which people distract themselves from seeking to satisfy this restlessness.

- What is your favorite story in the Gospels about a person who recognized the need for God's help?

- Paraphrase in your own words the quotation from Saint Augustine.

- Was there ever a time in your life when you felt a hunger for God? How was that hunger satisfied?

- People usually experience one of the four basic hungers—the need to love and be loved, the need to know, the need to grow, and the need to live forever—more than the others. At the present time, which need are you feeling the most?

Being Alone

To come to know their deepest need—to find God—people have to slow down. They have to be alone. They need to "go inside." They need solitude, even if it is only for a short time each day. Our lives are pushed and pulled into thousands of activities. We need a resting place where there is no pressure, or we will never come in contact with the deeper side of life or with our basic hunger. It is in this silence and openness that we begin to discover both our hunger and God as the answer to our deepest yearnings.

Most people at some time or other do stop and reflect on their lives, but usually they do not do it regularly on a daily basis. They resist setting aside time, not because they do not know their need and God's offer, but because they find it hard to break habits that keep them busy and distracted.

Most people have developed habits that keep them from stopping, being alone, and going inside. They involve themselves in work, making money, doing errands, keeping house. All these activities go at such a frantic pace that they find it impossible to break the chain with which these activities bind them.

Dependencies on things such as TV, radio, alcohol and other drugs, sex, and work make it almost impossible to be alone and go inside for an honest look at oneself.

People may also resist because of fear. There often is a hidden fear, never quite fully expressed or clear, of what they will discover if they begin to touch their deepest longings and face the rock-bottom questions about the direction and meaning of their lives. They fear that they may find nothing there, or that they will not like what they discover about themselves and will have to change something.

Not living up to our potential is the price we have to pay for not living a reflective life and simply taking things for granted. When we live this way, we may have a sense that life is meaningless and has no overriding purpose. We may be bored or anxious and feel that our lives are going nowhere fast.

- Reflect on a time when you were alone, and quiet, and in touch with your deeper self. Describe the experience. What did you see, hear, taste, smell, feel, think?

- How often do you take time to go inside your heart and to reflect quietly, instead of being caught up in the flurry of outside activities?

- What distractions keep you from having a fixed, daily time for reflection?

- What specific action do you need to take to set aside at least fifteen minutes of quiet time each day?

Practice

1. At this point on your journey, what is your deepest hunger?

_____

_____

_____

2. A simple way to become more conscious of the reality of God in your daily life is to set aside ten or fifteen minutes each day for yourself. Some people like to do this before going to bed at night. Others find that in order to find time they have to get up fifteen minutes earlier, before the usual activities of the day begin. Most people find it next to impossible to take time during the day to "go inside" and be alone with themselves. Here are some suggestions for your time alone:

   a. Find a quiet spot—away from the TV, the family, work, and other distractions.
   b. Relax, get comfortable, and open your mind and heart to God present with you.
   c. Be quiet in the presence of God and just listen to God
   · speaking to your heart.
   d. Hear the question Jesus asked the blind man in Mark 10:15, "What do you want me to do for you?" Then answer for yourself.

3. Another simple way to become more conscious of your need for God is to reflect on questions such as these:

   a. When during this day (or the previous day) have I felt closest to God?
   b. How have I experienced the presence and love of God in the events of the day?
   c. What did I hear God saying to me in the events of the day?
   d. What is happening in my life to make me more conscious of my need for God?

2

THE CALL TO TAKE A JOURNEY

People's efforts to meet their deepest needs, to satisfy their deepest hungers, can be compared to a journey. It is a gradual movement from being isolated and alienated to being in communion with themselves, with other people, and with God. They become more and more whole. They resolve more and more of the conflict of values within themselves. They gradually come to value, prize, and care for God and neighbor as much as for themselves.

Jesus told a story that helps clarify what this journey is all about:

> "A man had two sons. The younger of them said to his father, 'Father, give me the share of the estate that is coming to me.' So the father divided up the property. Some days later this younger son collected all his belongings and went off to a distant land, where he squandered his money on dissolute living."

In other words, the young man wanted to control his own life. He thought he knew what was best for him. He thought he knew what would make him happy. He isolated himself and alienated himself from his father. Then something happened.

> "After he had spent everything, a great famine broke out in that country and he was in dire need. So he attached himself to one of the propertied class of the place, who sent him to his farm to take care of the pigs. He longed to fill his belly with the husks that were fodder for the pigs but no one made a move to give him anything."

Now, he was alienated not only from his father but also from himself and everyone else. He reached a crisis, and he began to dialogue with himself. He came to his senses and realized the reality of where he was and of what he had done.

He assessed the situation and saw that there was nothing there for him. His spiritual journey began.

> *"Coming to his senses at last, he said: 'How many hired hands at my father's place have more than enough to eat, while here I am starving! I will break away and return to my father, and say to him, Father, I have sinned against God and against you; I no longer deserve to be called your son. Treat me like one of your hired hands.'"*

Luke 15:11–19

Coming to this realization must have been difficult for that young man. He must have suffered a great deal of mental anguish, but he made the choice and set off for his father's house. The journey home must have seemed much longer than the first journey, to the distant land, because he did not know what he was going to find when he got home. But, as we know, there was a happy ending. The father welcomed him with open arms, paid no attention to his protestations of unworthiness, even threw a party for him and took him back into a full place in the family.

The starting point of our journey may not be as dramatic as that of the prodigal son, but anyone who is serious about satisfying the deep hunger in his or heart in one way or another has to come to his or her senses. There comes a time when we are no longer satisfied where we are. The isolation and alienation we feel are so great that we know our relationships with ourselves, with others, and with Good need to change.

- Recall a time in your life when you had the experience of coming to your senses and realizing that what you were doing or thinking or feeling was destructive to you or to someone else. What brought you to your senses?

- How did you feel?

- What did you do?

Basic Attitudes toward the Journey

An attitude is simply a way of seeing life, a pattern of thinking about people and events, that directs the course of a person's life. People's attitudes, more than their ideas and ideals, affect the choices they make, the direction they take.

There are two very different attitudes we can choose about this spiritual journey. Our decision will affect how we see God and how we act. One possibility is to think of the spiritual life as a call to be perfect. Seeking perfection, if by perfection we mean a finished product, is not a very helpful attitude, because it implies a goal that is static and closed. When we think of perfection in this way, we too easily see life as a question of black and white. We tend to think of ourselves and of others as either good or bad, in the state of grace or in the state of sin. In this view, if there is any movement in our lives, it is like jumping in and out of the pool of grace or bouncing on or off the trampoline of sin. We tend to see God as a judge and a scorekeeper, and judge ourselves by how perfectly we keep the rules. If we do keep them, we think of ourselves as having arrived, as being among the saved.

The other possibility is to think of the spiritual life as a process, a pilgrimage or journey that is never finished as long as we are breathing. With this attitude, we see both good and bad in ourselves. We realize that we are neither good nor bad, but someplace in-between. We are conscious that both grace and sin are working in us, that we are far from finished products, that we always have the potential for more growth. We recognize that sin is part and parcel of our journey, but we do not see sin as a sign of total failure. Rather, we see sin as a part of a larger reality, of a greater redemptive story. We realize that the only fatal mistake is stopping on our journey, because stopping leads to stagnation, even to spiritual death.

When Peter saw Jesus transfigured on the mountain, he wanted to erect three tents and stay there (see Mark 9:2–8). But he, like Jesus, still had a long and painful way to go on his journey. The reply Peter received to his suggestion was simply, "This is my Son, my beloved. Listen to him." Jesus told Peter and the others that he was on the final leg of his journey. He was on his way to Jerusalem, where he would suffer and die. Peter may not have realized it at the time, but

17

he and the others had a long way to go before they could rest peacefully in the presence of Moses, Elijah, and the Lord.

Seeing our spiritual life as a journey frees us from the constraint to be perfect, or at least cleaned up, before we approach God. We realize that mistakes and sins are not fatal. We are free to grow from our experience, both good and bad. We realize that where we are on our journey should never be a stopping place. With this attitude, we see God as a companion on our journey who calls us to go beyond the law, submitting ourselves to God's will in loving trust and hope.

- What are some of the things your parents said or did that told you that you ought to be perfect?

- What are some areas in your life now where you feel that you ought to be perfect?

- How do you feel when you do not live up to your own expectations or to others' expectations that you be perfect?

- How could seeing spiritual growth as a journey, rather than as striving for perfection, help you in your efforts to satisfy your deepest hunger?

A Journey with God

The spiritual journey is a journey of relationships, a journey on which a person grows closer to God or further from God, depending on how he or she relates to others. Many people instinctively think of the journey as an *intrapersonal* project— a trip into themselves, a journey to explore themselves, improve themselves, and so become better and holier in God's eyes. But the spiritual journey is *not* simply an intrapersonal process, something confined to self-improvement. It is an *interpersonal* process by which people deepen and strengthen their relationships with God and with others, as well as with themselves. Jesus put it simply: "Treat others the way you would have them treat you; this sums up the law and the prophets" *(Matthew 7:12).* " 'You shall love the Lord your God with your whole heart, with your whole soul, and with all your mind.' This is the greatest and first commandment. The second is like it: 'You shall love your neighbor as yourself.' On these two commandments the whole law is based, and the prophets as well" *(Matthew 22:37–39).*

We are called to be in a covenant with God, a pact of lasting, loving fidelity. This relationship can best be described as an invitation to share the very life of God. God is not merely "out there" running this universe and waiting for us to call God to come down and enter into our lives. God, who is love, total, complete, and absolute, is already present in the depths of our being with forgiveness and power to transform. The relationship God calls us to is one of opening ourselves to that love, that forgiveness, that transforming power. It is a process by which we gradually break down the barriers within us so that God's love, God's forgiveness, God's transforming power can flow more and more in our lives. As the God-life becomes more and more operative in us, as our lives blend with God's more and more, we are impelled to move out of ourselves and enter into relationships with other people, in order to help them free themselves from the restraints that imprison God's love, forgiveness, and transforming power within them.

This journey into deeper and deeper relationships is not easy. It is marked by struggle. If we focus simply on ourselves, the struggle will always be within and with ourselves. We will become more and more self-centered. If our journey focuses on our relationships with God and others, then the struggle will be to connect with and respond to the others in our relationships. We will find a wider and wider world in which we can walk in love and forgiveness and transforming power.

- To get a sense of what is involved in an intimate relationship, think of a close friendship. Name the friend.

- When and how did the friendship begin?

- What are two or three events that have cemented that friendship over the years?

- What are two or three situations that have strained that friendship?

- How has this relationship affected the way you see yourself, others, and God?

The First Step: Trust in God

The spiritual journey is not clearly marked. People are not always sure of the direction they should take. They may stumble, take detours, miss the signs, and even have to retrace their steps. But they trust that God is with them even in these false steps, inspiring, guiding, correcting so that the general direction of their lives is growth in relationship with the Lord and with their neighbors.

The journey is not a solitary one that we have to make alone. In our efforts to grow spiritually we have the help, the example, the prayers, the guidance of the Church, the Christian community of which we are a part. Even though each of us goes to God in our own way, we also go with others as a member of a community.

Mary, the first member of the community, is a prime example of this growth. Even though Mary's journey was always in accordance with the will of God, she had to grow in her understanding of and in her response to God's will. The stories in the Gospel which speak of her show her as a young girl afraid yet courageously responsive to God's call, a young mother caring for her child, a mother confused and wondering about her lost son, a mother who must let go of her son as he goes about his public ministry, a mother who must watch her son die, and, finally, a mother, confirmed in Easter faith, who waits for the coming of the Pentecost Spirit. Mary experienced her call as a gradually unfolding process, a journey, not unlike the one we are called to make.

In most journeys, the end is not determined by the way one gets there. If New York is the destination, when a person arrives, it makes little difference whether he or she flew, took the train, drove, or walked. New York is still the same. But the spiritual journey is different. The end of the journey is determined by the quality of the journey itself.

In one view of the spiritual life, what comes after death is all-important, and the goal of life is getting through the pearly gates, even if it is a last-minute dash. But when we see the spiritual life as a journey, the way we live each day is all-important, because we see life after death as a continuation of the way we live our relationships with ourselves, with others, and with God day by day.

- Many people see their lives as a series of isolated incidents with no direction. To help you see the patterns in your own journey, reflect on one important aspect of your life, such as career, marriage, or education. What aspect of your life will you trace?

- When did it begin? Where did you want to go?

- When has it been smooth sailing?

- When have there been rough spots, roadblocks, detours?

- When has the direction of this journey changed?

- Who are the people who have helped you on the journey?

21

- What people or circumstances have hindered you on the journey?

- How have you felt at different times on this journey?

- How worthwhile has this journey been for you?

- What pattern, if any, do you see in this journey?

- What direction do you see your life in this area taking now?

Practice

1. At this point on your journey, in what direction would you like to move?

_____

_____

_____

2. It is usually helpful to share the story of your spiritual journey with a spiritual companion, one who will help you claim it as your own and who will help you get insights into the direction of that journey. The great masters of the spiritual life have said that such a companion is necessary on the journey. Jesus sent his disciples out two by two; they were a support to one another.

   Seek a spiritual companion for your journey. Agree to this relationship for a specific period, such as three months, and set a regular time to meet. This companion must be someone you can trust with the secrets of your heart and someone with whom you can be completely open and honest. Such a relationship is a risk, but it is worth trying.

3

SPEAK, LORD!

Good communication is a way of deepening one's relationship with another. Sharing memories, feelings, thoughts brings people closer together. Communicating ordinary and extraordinary moments on a regular basis is essential for a good relationship. The deeper and more complete the communication, the deeper and firmer the relationship.

Communication is a two-way street. One speaks, the other listens—but listens so as to hear everything the speaker is saying. Then the other responds to what is being said. If one is preoccupied with one's own thoughts or with what one wants to say, then one cannot hear the other. If both are trying to speak at the same time, then neither can be heard.

To deepen our union with God, regular communication is essential. Spiritual development involves listening to God. The spiritual journey demands that we sharpen our ability to hear God's word. We need to become more and more conscious that God is communicating all day long. Those who take the spiritual journey seriously usually have no trouble believing that God hears them and understands what they are trying to say. Their difficulty usually lies in becoming aware of the many ways God speaks to them and in listening to what God is saying.

God speaks to us in many ways each day. In fact, nothing happens that cannot be the voice of God speaking to us, if we but listen carefully. God speaks to us through other people. God is revealed through the events of daily life—even through sin, failure, and disaster. God's voice is heard in music, sculpture, painting, architecture, and poetry. At times, God's words are found in our own mental processes. At other times, we hear God in the quiet of our deepest selves.

Moses and Joshua, the first great leaders of the Hebrews, were very conscious of the fact that God was revealed to the Hebrews through the events of history. At the end of his life, Moses recited a song for the whole of Israel to hear. In it, he spoke of how God had been revealed through the events of their liberation from Egypt. He said, "God found them in a wilderness, a wasteland of howling desert. God shielded them and cared for them, guarding them as the apple of God's eye. . . . God had them ride triumphant over the summits of the land and live off the products of its fields" (Deuteronomy 32:10, 13).

At the end of his life Joshua spoke in a similar vein:

> "You have seen all that the Lord, your God, has done for you against all these nations; for it has been the Lord, your God, who fought for you. . . . At your approach the Lord has driven out large and strong nations, and to this day no one has withstood you. One of you puts to flight a thousand, because it is the Lord, your God, who fights for you as God promised you."
>
> Joshua 23:3, 9–10

- When have you heard God speak to you through an event in your life?

- When have you heard God speak to you by the words or actions of another person?

- When have you heard God speak to you in the very depths of your being?

- When have you heard God speak to you through nature?

- When have you heard God speak to you through art or music?

- When you need to hear the voice of God, where do you go and what do you do?

A Message for You

Among the many ways God communicates with us, the Scriptures have a special position. Our knowledge of God, God's thoughts about human beings, God's ways of showing love and concern for people are recorded in the Scriptures. Anyone aspiring to a fuller relationship with God must be attentive to the Scriptures. For Christians, Scriptures have been and always will be the foundation for coming to know and hear the Lord.

The Scriptures should be read as a personal letter written to us. Significant letters that we have received often hold a meaning that moves beyond the immediate circumstances in which they were written. We keep returning to them time and time again with the expectation that they will cast light on our current situation.

The Scriptures—even though they speak about people and events long past—are addressed to us and speak to us about our lives. When we read the history of Israel, we are reading not only about the adventures of an ancient people, removed far from our experience, but also about the loving care God has for us here and now. When we read of Jesus curing the sick and calming the sea, we see the power of God at work through him to conquer the evil and the ills we are heir to, and we realize that this same power is now available to us in and through the Holy Spirit who lives in us.

The Scriptures are not like a letter from a parent to a child telling that child all the answers to his or her questions. The Scriptures do not provide a way of bypassing ordinary human knowledge or of solving scientific, political, or historical problems. They are words written in love that challenge the way we think, the values we hold, the courses of action we follow. They are meant to give us new vision and, most importantly, new hope.

Therefore, it is imperative not to take the Bible in a naively literal way, that is, without appreciating the meaning of the words in their historical and literary context. It is dangerous and distorting to read the Bible as if it were this morning's newspaper. These books were written in another time, by people who lived in a different culture and whose thought patterns and literary patterns were different from today's. To hear what the Lord is saying, we cannot take one quotation by itself. We need to take the words and events in the context of the whole Bible. In our desire to hear God's word in the Scriptures, we need to learn more about the times and the situations in which the books were written. We will then see that what seems like history most often is not history as the modern reader knows it, but a theological statement, a theological story, with a very profound message for people today.

The Bible is complicated. It needs to be interpreted, and at times it is difficult to understand. But we can begin to read and profit from the parts that do make sense to us, that do not seem to be too complicated or difficult. In time, the desire to hear what God is saying should cause us to want to know the Bible better. With the help of the Spirit, of the Church, and of biblical scholars, we will begin to recognize more clearly what God is communicating to us through the Bible.

- Can you recall a story or a passage from the Scriptures in which you felt that God was talking to you?

- On a scale from 0 to 10 (10 being the highest), how important is reading the Scriptures in your life?

- What difficulties do you encounter in reading the Scriptures?

- Where do you go for help in understanding the Scriptures?

Practice

1. At this point on your journey, what do you want from the Scriptures?

_____

_____

_____

2. There are many ways to read the Scriptures. One way may appeal to you more at one time in life than at another. For example, at times, the developing history of God's people will intrigue you. At other times, you will want to see how the great basic themes in the Bible gradually develop. You may become interested in the characters in the stories and in their very human psychological processes. It matters little which approach you take, as long as you keep in mind that the Scriptures are the communication of a loving God, given to you in many forms through the words of human authors.

    Below are just a few of the ways people have found to get into the Scriptures and listen to what God is saying. Try one until you become comfortable with it. Then, try another way.

    a. Begin by reading one book of the Bible as you would read any other book. Identify the characters, the point of the book, the plot. Often reading all the way through one book gives one an entirely different perspective of it.

    b. As you read, use a good commentary to help you see how the sections you are reading might apply to your own life.

    c. Take the three lectionary readings from the coming Sunday's liturgy and read them two or three times during the week. As you read, ask yourself, ''What is the challenge in these passages for me? What questions do they raise about my life? What do they mean to me?'' In this way, you are prepared to listen to God's word at the liturgy and to hear how the preacher interprets it.

d. Begin reading a section of a book and keep reading it until something strikes you. Close the book; reflect on the verse or verses that struck you; pray over them; keep recalling them during the rest of the day.

e. Read one of the parables or narratives. Picture yourself as one of the people in the story. Then get in touch with your feelings and thoughts as the one in the story. Hear the words as being spoken directly to you. Look at your own life, and see how you are like the person in the story. Ask yourself what your feelings and thoughts are, and what the words in the Scriptures say to you about your situation. Then have a conversation with Jesus or with God about your life.

f. Realize that the section or passage you are reading is actually a love letter to you from God. Summarize it in one sentence spoken by God to you.

4

REACHING OUT TO GOD

In all significant relationships, people feel the need to reach out to the other. They reach out to those they care about in little rituals such as exchanging valentines and birthday gifts. They reach out in intense and heart-to-heart conversations. On rare occasions, they pass beyond the intensity of words and communicate soul to soul, perhaps in silence or only in an embrace. In the same way, people yearn to be in contact with God, to feel God's presence, and so they reach out to God. Reaching out to God—by simple rituals, by words, by silence—is what we call prayer. This is our response to God, who is continually reaching out to us in the daily events of our lives.

The conviction that prayer is necessary is the foundation of the Christian's spiritual journey. Without prayer, a person can get to know him or herself better and may be able to acknowledge the existence of a Supreme Being or give intellectual assent to a creed. But without prayer, the person cannot grow in a personal relationship with God.

The evangelists, especially Saint Luke, tell us that Jesus frequently went off to pray. Prayer was the foundation of the spiritual journey of Jesus. He spoke frequently about his relationship to God. The disciples of Jesus found his way of relating to God and of praying very attractive. They wanted to pray in the same way, so that they would have the same type of relationship. "One day he [Jesus] was praying in a certain place. When he had finished, one of his disciples asked him, 'Lord, teach us to pray, as John taught his disciples'" (Luke 11:1).

Those early Christians who believed in Jesus believed in reaching out to God in prayer. Saint Paul encouraged his friends in Thessalonica to "pray always." In his letter to the Romans, he acknowledged that people do not always know how to pray and that they needed help in praying. But he wrote that the help they needed was always at hand:

The Spirit too helps us in our weakness, for we do not know how to pray as we ought; but the Spirit makes intercession for us with groanings that cannot be expressed in speech. The God who searches hearts knows what the Spirit means, for the Spirit intercedes for the saints as God wills.

Romans 8:26–27

- Recall a time when someone reached out to you in love by a gift, by words, by a silent embrace. What happened? How did you feel?

- What did the incident say to you about the relationship?

- Think about a time you reached out to someone. What did you do? How did you feel?

- What did you learn about the relationship?

- What do these incidents suggest to you about prayer?

One-to-One Prayer

Spiritual writers divide prayer into many different categories. A simple division is to look at prayer either as one-to-one, the prayer a person does by him or herself, or as many-to-one, the prayer a person does with others. One-to-one prayer has three expressions:

1. We reach out to God by saying prayers we were taught, by reciting the formulas we have memorized.
2. We reach out to God and speak to God in our own words. This form of prayer very often comes from reading and reflecting on the Scriptures or some spiritual book.
3. We reach out to God heart to heart in the language of silence, in the language of the heart.

Each of these forms of personal prayer serves us well at different times in our lives, and we may well use all three on the same day. In no way are they exclusive. Actually they can feed into one another and enhance one another. Each expression has advantages and dangers.

Reciting prayers that we have memorized can be of great comfort. They are familiar. They are available. We can "hook into them." They can carry us along in periods of dryness. Although they do not usually carry a high emotional charge, they help us realize that we need to keep in touch with God. We feel that these prayers belong to us, even though we did not create them. When the disciples asked Jesus to teach them how to pray, he did not give them a series of exercises to do for meditation or teach them a method of prayer. He gave them a formula, a very simple formula: "Father, hallowed be your name, your kingdom come. Give us each day our daily bread. Forgive us our sins for we too forgive all who do us wrong; and subject us not to the trial" (Luke 11:2–4).

Periodically, we need to renew the practice of "saying prayers." However, merely reciting the words can degenerate into mumbo jumbo, the kind of babbling in prayer against which Jesus warned. Saying special formulas a specific number of times can be a way of trying to manipulate divine power to get something, rather than being a genuine reaching out to God. If "said" prayers become a mindless recitation of words or if they assume a magical quality, we will stunt our spiritual growth and make little or no progress on the spiritual journey.

The key to transforming familiar prayers into more than an automatic recitation of words is taking time to consider what we are saying. We have to note where our heart is when we say them. For example, the Lord's Prayer, which most of us learned before we were capable of understanding the depths of meaning in it, can be rediscovered and revitalized by saying it thoughtfully and slowly, savoring the meaning of the words. When we join the human experiences of suffering, loss, or joy to the slow and thoughtful praying of the Lord's Prayer, our eyes will begin to see new dimensions of God's will and of the coming of God's rule in our lives. We will become more trusting of God's daily care for us. We will realize that God forgives us and that an essential condition for the spiritual journey is that we forgive others. In fact, after prayerful reflection on the meaning of the Lord's Prayer, we may find that it is the best and most comforting prayer we can say as we make our way along the path of life.

- Which memorized prayers do you usually say and when do you say them?

- Recall one experience when a memorized prayer—the Our Father, the rosary, a psalm—meant a great deal to you. What was the occasion?

- When you use memorized prayers, what feelings— closeness to God, joy, love, obligation, dullness, routine— do you experience?

- How important are memorized prayers in your efforts to communicate with God?

Spontaneous Prayer

Spontaneous prayer is the natural response of the heart to the presence of God. It may arise as a result of perceiving God's hand in nature or in some event in a person's life. Often it arises from the need for help in a situation. A spontaneous reaching out to God in a person's own words, or even in pregnant silence, often is the result of reading and reflection on the Scriptures, some spiritual book, or some event in life.

The danger with spontaneous prayer is that it can become too restricted, limited primarily to our own needs or the needs of those close to us. We may skip over our need to be thankful, to praise God, and to ask for forgiveness. We may even confuse reading and reflecting on the meaning of Scripture or of a book with praying. Then the method which should lead into prayer becomes the object of our activity. To overcome this danger, we must open our hearts and minds to see the larger picture of God's world and of God's love. In this way, we can talk to God about the needs and the concerns of all God's people.

- What was the most memorable time when you talked to God in your own words? How did you feel?

- How often during the day do you talk with God in your own words?

- What has been your experience of talking to God in your own words after reading the Scriptures or a book?

Prayer of the Heart

The third form of one-to-one prayer could well be called "prayer of the heart." It is a deeply personal prayer born of a person's solitude and interior life. So quite naturally it speaks the language of silence, the language of the heart. This form of reaching out to God is *not* mysterious, remote, or limited to a few chosen people.

A great mystic of the sixteenth century, Saint Theresa of Avila, called this form of prayer mental prayer. She wrote, "To my mind, mental prayer is nothing else than taking time

35

frequently to be alone with the one we know who loves us." She said that prayer is a matter of time, presence, solitude, and experiencing love. She did not hope for special results, for gratifying mystical experiences, or even for feelings of consolation from this form of prayer.

Many of us have reached out to God in this way already. We can identify moments when "nothing special" happened, but when we had a sense of the presence of God. This form of prayer is satisfying because we know with our heart that we are loved and that we in turn love.

This kind of prayer is simple, but the complication of our lives makes it difficult for us to be at peace with ourselves so that we can enter into true solitude. It is not an easy thing for us—surrounded as we are by countless noises—to sit quietly and wait. It is not easy for us—people who are geared to be productive and not to waste time—to be present and expect "nothing" to happen as a result of our presence.

Many of us find great difficulty with reaching out to God in the simple, quiet prayer of the heart. We find it most difficult to shift gears and go from living frantically, productively, noisily, always conscious of time, to being quiet, peaceful, open to whatever God wants. We need some form of discipline that goes counter to the hurly-burly mood of our culture. We need to practice some kind of introductory method as a prelude to the prayer of the heart. We need to learn "how to be" in a simple and quiet way so that we can be with and for the Lord.

Psalm 24 challenges us to the openness needed to experience prayer of the heart. It pictures the person who is ready to receive God:

> Who can ascend the mountain of the Lord?
>   or who may stand in God's holy place?
> Those whose hands are sinless, whose hearts are clean,
>   who desire not what is vain,
>   nor swear deceitfully to their neighbors.
> They shall receive a blessing from the Lord,
>   a reward from God their savior.
> Such is the race that seeks for God,
>   that seeks the face of the God of Jacob.
>
> Psalm 24:3–6

- Recall a time when you stood in the presence of God and experienced prayer of the heart. What was the occasion?

- How did you feel during and after this experience?

- What blessing did you receive from the experience?

Many-to-One Prayer

On the great and exciting journey of which we have been speaking, we are not isolated individuals, each groping our own lonely way on our own separate paths. Even though each person's journey is unique, we still are on a common journey with others. With them we reach out to God. With them we encounter Father, Son, and Holy Spirit in various ways. We can call this common reaching out to God the many-to-one form of prayer, or the "prayer of encounter," because Jesus promised, "Where two or three of you are gathered in my name, there I am in their midst" (Matthew 18:20). In meeting one another, believers meet the Lord. When believers gather, Jesus is present and praying with them. He is part of the many who are reaching out to the Father.

This prayer of encounter takes many different forms. When people gather to celebrate the Eucharist, they meet the Lord not only as individuals but as a group. The individual's voice is joined to that of the group. The individual's needs are joined to the needs of all the others in the group. Together, all those present and the entire Church reach out to the Lord in response to the Lord's reaching into their lives. Because the believers are gathered by the power of the Holy Spirit, what happens when they come together is more than the sum of their human effort.

37

Sometimes people find it difficult to meet God through a formal religious ritual because the words and actions are foreign to their experience. The words of the ritual are not their own, are not spoken by them, and are not understood by them. They do not understand the symbolism, the metaphors, the background of the words and actions. They are looking to get something from the service, but what they expect is too little—good music, an inspiring sermon. They have not yet discovered that ritual offers them something greater—an encounter in which the living Lord and the Christian reach out to one another in love, in care, in trust.

Besides formal religious moments, the prayer of encounter happens in other settings—for example, when friends gather, share Scripture and life experiences, and pray together. The prayer of encounter does not even require anything as formal as a prayer group. When people simply gather and are attentive to one another in love and compassion, they experience the presence of God. This form of encountering God may be more evident in those moments that people consider to be ministry or a kind of formal service they render to one another. But friendships can also be moments of disclosure of God's love for them and of their reaching out to God. Wrapped in the human and limited experience of love is the ground of all love—God.

Many-to-one prayer has to be cultivated in the same way as one-to-one prayer. We need to reflect on the meaning of the words and actions of the formal rituals. We have to learn how to be open and ready to meet other people so that in less structured and more informal ways together we can reach out to God.

- Recall a moving experience you had praying with other people. What was the occasion?

- How did you feel?

- What did you learn about prayer from this experience?

- How have liturgical celebrations been a form of prayer for you?

- What do you like about formal, liturgical celebrations?

- What do you dislike about formal, liturgical celebrations?

Practice

1. At this point on your journey, how would you like to change or improve your prayer life?

2. You probably have a favorite way of reaching out to God. This may be saying learned prayers slowly and thoughtfully. It may be time spent with others at the liturgy or at prayer groups. It may be the quiet time when you are simply present to God. But it is essential that you have definite and focused contact time with the Lord.

   It may also be necessary to learn simple methods or disciplines that will make your prayer more of a genuine reaching out to God. To do this, you first have to be clear about which forms of prayer you use, when you use them, and how you use them. You need to be clear about your expectations of prayer and your attitude toward prayer. Then you need to identify your feelings when you pray. If you have this information and feel that something is lacking, you are ready to try some different ways of approaching prayer.

   First, consider prayer formulas, such as memorized prayers or the prayers of the liturgy. Take them apart phrase by phrase and reflect on how each phrase relates to what is going on in your life. For example, look at the Lord's Prayer. Take each phrase and ask yourself questions such as these:

   a. What things going on in my life help me realize that God's rule has indeed come into my life?
   b. What are two or three things I need as daily bread?
   c. Whom do I need to forgive, and for what do I need to be forgiven?
   d. What are the evils from within or from without that are threatening to destroy me and from which I need to be delivered?

Do this simple activity with your family, two or three friends, or a prayer group. Learn from each other what the words of the prayer mean in your lives.

Use the same process with the prayers of the Mass, especially the various eucharistic prayers. Take them apart phrase by phrase, not once or twice but several times. Ask, "What do the words mean in my life?" If you find that you do not understand them, or if you find that they do not seem to relate to your life, learn a little more about them.

Second, consider spontaneous one-to-one prayers. Read a passage of Scripture and underline the words that strike you. Reflect on them and then talk one-to-one to God about your thoughts and feelings.

Finally, consider the prayer of encounter. Here one has to learn the discipline of letting go and becoming quiet so heart can touch heart. One way of doing this is to sit in a comfortable position, both feet planted on the floor, hands relaxed on your knees. Slowly take in a deep breath, hold it for the count of seven, then slowly let it out. Do this three times until you feel relaxation flowing through your body. Then be quiet. Here is an image that may help clear and quiet your mind. Picture a beautiful green lawn covered with leaves. Then feel a gentle wind blowing them away until the lawn is perfectly clean and empty.

There are many other forms of relaxing exercises and centering practices that can help you become quiet inside so that God can speak and you can hear.

5

COMPANIONS ON THE JOURNEY

One of the exciting features of reading the Bible is looking behind the incidents and words to see that the people in the Bible struggled with the same joys, feelings, and problems that we do. We realize that the processes going on in our lives were also at work in theirs. In other words, they were on the same spiritual journey we are on.

In the lives of the Apostles, we can see that they were making the same journey to become Church that we have to make. There are enough incidents in the Gospels to show that they went through the same basic steps we do. They were a rather ordinary mix of people ranging from Nathanael, "a true Israelite in whom there is no guile" *(John 1:45–49)* to Levi, or Matthew, a "sinner," a social outcast, a tax collector for the Romans (see Luke 5:27–29). In different ways, they received a call to deepen their relationship with God. Peter, Andrew, James, and John were called from their fishing boats (see Matthew 4:18–22), Nathanael from his rest under the tree, Matthew from his tax collector's table. To have been receptive to the call, they must have felt dissatisfied with their lives and drawn to seek something better than they had. They had to be searching.

They made the choice to follow Jesus, to talk with him, to listen to what he had to say, and to reach out to others. When he chose them out of all his disciples to become a core community with him, they were free to accept his invitation or not. In the three years they were with Jesus on earth, they were gradually drawn into a fuller realization of God's plan for them. As Jews they already knew that they related to God as a community, a chosen people, and that God expected them to relate to one another in a special way. From Jesus they began to see and hear a new dimension of what it means to have God as the only center of one's life. They saw in Jesus one who gave himself without reservation to the will of God.

They saw in him values different from those espoused by the community in which they lived—values such as unconditional love, unconditional forgiveness, willingness to share one's gifts for the benefit of others, and willingness to accept the suffering that came with that sharing.

At the same time, they had to decide whether they wanted these values for themselves and whether they wanted to continue the journey with this particular group of people, with this community. We know of one who chose not to do so, Judas (see Matthew 26:3–16). We know that the Apostles did not see and accept the whole picture at once. James and John were anxious to see their own personal ambitions fulfilled, although Jesus had spoken of a serving and self-forgetting way of life (see Mark 10:35–45). Nevertheless, in spite of difficulties and a lack of full understanding, eleven of the twelve and many of the disciples decided to follow Jesus and draw others into this community of followers.

- Images and pictures often express a person's thoughts and feelings better than words. Draw two pictures—one of the Church as you saw and experienced it years ago and the other as you see and experience it today. Do not worry about your artistic ability. Use simple lines, symbols, stick figures.

- List some of the things that caused the change in your perception of the Church.

An Imperfect Community

A careful reading of the Acts of the Apostles and of the Epistles shows that the early Christian communities were not ideal. Peter and Paul argued. Paul rejected Mark for being a coward. The Corinthians got drunk at the Eucharist. The rich did not always share with the poor. Nevertheless they saw that their relationship with Jesus required their relationship with one another. They had to form a community, a church.

Our call is not only to make a journey to God, a journey on which we seek a personal, life-changing, fulfilling relationship with God. It is also a call to seek companions who share a vision of life expressed in common beliefs and common values. Although God looks deep into our souls and quietly issues a very personal invitation, "I want *you* as a friend," God also draws us into community and says, "I want you to become *one of my people*." God calls us to become Church.

- In order to have a realistic appreciation of where you are on your journey of becoming Church, you need to think about your relationship to the Church. What have been the high points and the low points of the relationship? When has the Church been important in your life? When has it not been important?

- Think of your present parish and of various parishes of which you have been a member. Draw a life line representing your life in the Church. Have the line go up for positive experiences and go down for negative ones. Indicate what each high and each low symbolizes.

Our Call to Community

Our response to this invitation is at once highly personal and profoundly communal. In one sense, each person has to make the journey alone. All the physical, environmental, and experiential elements that come together to constitute a person's life will never come together again to make an exact replica of that person. On the other hand, enough of these elements are so alike that the person needs to make the journey with others.

This gathering of like believers is the Church, the social setting for our spiritual journey. When we use the word *Church,* we are speaking of various groups with whom we are related, some more closely and other less closely. The word may mean a small group of people who know each other well, pray together, and care for one another. It may mean a parish in which people know some other people, pray in large gatherings, and are concerned about a few. It may also mean the universal Church, in which we are in touch with believers throughout the world. Our connection with the totality of fellow believers is a common faith, common sacraments, common Scriptures, and for Catholics, a common authority—the pope and the bishops.

This universal Church also puts us in touch with the people of faith through the centuries who have walked the journey in hope and who have been guided by the promises of the one God. This Church passes on to us the beliefs, values, and traditions of generations of people who have made the choice to follow the Lord. The Church preserves for us the distilled wisdom of their efforts to enter into and deepen their relationship with God. This wisdom growing from the faith of the community may challenge views and values that we and our culture treasure. The Church exists not only to sustain and nourish us but also to question our habitual and comfortable ways of thinking and acting.

- Where is the Church most real for you?

- If you belong to a small group whom you consider to be Church, what has been your experience with this group?

- Has the faith of the Church challenged your values? How did you respond?

A Personal Decision

Sometime on our journey we have to come to grips with the Church. For most of us, the decision whether or not to belong to the Church was made for us early in life by someone else. If our parents made the choice to bring us into the community by having us baptized, receive the Eucharist, and be confirmed, we had little to say about it. Nevertheless, the Church was the matrix in which we learned how to relate to God, how to pray, how to hear the word of God. As adults, if we are seriously seeking a deeper relationship with God, we have to face the question of the Church. We have to face the dissonance between the ideal of Church and the reality of Church that we have experienced. We have to face our expectations of Church and our experience of how those expectations have been fulfilled. We have to ask ourselves whether our expectations are realistic.

- At what time in your life did you decide *for yourself* that you wanted to be a member of the Church? How did this come about?

- Why are you still in the Church?

- Listed below are some of the ways the Church may help a person on his or her spiritual journey. Rank each one from 1 to 4 according to how you experience the Church helping you. The numeral *1* means "Very Much"; the numeral *2*, "Somewhat"; the numeral *3*, "Little"; the numeral *4*, "None."

  ____ Telling clearly what you should believe
  ____ Presenting clear rules of right and wrong
  ____ Giving strong leadership
  ____ Helping you grow through liturgy and prayer opportunities
  ____ Being involved in social problems
  ____ Caring for your physical or psychological needs
  ____ Teaching Scripture
  ____ Giving you a sense of community

The Vision of Church

In the last generation, there have been great changes in the way people perceive the Church and in their expectations of it. The documents of Vatican Council II used fifteen or twenty different metaphors to describe it. They all say in one way or another that the Church is a community of people having the same faith and gathered together by the power of the Holy Spirit.

The Church mirrors the very God by whom we live and toward whom we move. God is a God of community, the Trinity, one God and Three Persons. Just as the relationship between Father and Son generates the Holy Spirit, so Christian life generates a community with a common life. In this vision, the Church is a community that offers people encouragement, challenge, and support as they progress on the journey of deepening their relationship with God and neighbor.

This is the ideal. But ideals have to be made concrete, and here we bump into the expectations of people. People see different ways in which the ideal can be realized. Some people see the Church as fulfilling its function best when it is tightly organized, with a uniform message and a clear-cut list of what is right and what is wrong. Others feel the Church best fulfills its role when it generates a sense of belonging in a warm, comforting group of like believers or when it promotes the prayer life of the community by a meaningful celebration of the liturgy. Some think it should primarily be preaching the Gospel. Others feel that the role of the Church is to battle social injustice or to meet the physical and psychological needs of people.

All of these views are part of the truth, but no one of them is the complete picture. Each has its strengths and weaknesses. A person's spiritual journey can easily go astray if he or she follows the clear, broad way of one view or of one's own expectations of what the Church should be. Many travel this road. But if only one view prevailed, the Church would not be truly catholic (open to all people) or holy (assisting all on their journey toward God) or one (having unity but not uniformity) or apostolic (reaching back to its roots in Christ and the Apostles, living in the present, and stretching toward the future).

When a person's spiritual journey is on the rough, narrow road leading to the narrow gate, it takes into account all views of the Church and people's differing expectations. The road is rough, because the best any community, large or small, can do is try to achieve a balance, realizing at the same time that it will always be in imbalance.

- Make a list of the various kinds of people in your parish (for example, children, old people, the sick, the widowed, etc.). Next to each item, jot down a few words indicating what you think they expect from the parish.

- What are the strengths and weaknesses of having a variety of people with a variety of expectations in a parish?

- How does your uniqueness contribute to building up the parish?

Practice

1. At this point on your journey, how would you like to improve your relationship to the Church?

_____

_____

_____

2. God chose you and gave you unique gifts. It is only by sharing your gifts with others on the journey that you find fulfillment. In this way, the community is built up. Saint Paul spoke eloquently about sharing gifts. Read these passages: Romans 12:3–8, 1 Corinthians 12:4–11, and Ephesians 4:11–13. Then spend a little time reflecting on these questions:

   a. What unique gifts have I been given?

   _____

   _____

   _____

   b. How can I share my gifts with others in the parish?

   _____

   _____

   _____

   c. What gifts do people in the parish have to share with me?

   _____

   _____

   _____

d. What can I do to be more open to accepting other people and their gifts and so help them grow?

_____

_____

_____

6

THE STRUGGLE OF THE JOURNEY

There are many journey stories in Scripture, illumining different facets of the spiritual journey. In Genesis 32:23-33, we read that Jacob was traveling home from a foreign land where he had acquired two wives, eleven children, and a large herd of sheep and goats. His family had gone on ahead. He was alone. In the dark, he met a stranger, and the two of them wrestled all night. The stranger could not prevail, and Jacob refused to end the bout till he had received a blessing. The stranger, whom Jacob identified with God, did bless him. But before he left, he struck Jacob on the hip. From that day on Jacob limped.

This story makes it clear that a spiritual journey is not always smooth and uneventful. Much of what happens on such a journey is cause for celebration: Jacob had acquired a family and great possessions. There are also obstacles on this journey, and a person has to struggle to overcome them, as Jacob did. A person may be wounded on the journey, as Jacob was, but he or she can recover and discover that the wound was a blessing.

A person may try to deny that the obstacles exist or attribute them to some other person or to some other cause. A person may try to avoid the struggle to remove them by plunging into some kind of feverish activity or by procrastinating about taking action. But until a person acknowledges the obstacles and wrestles with them hand to hand, there will be little growth in his or her relationship to God and neighbor. The person may not succeed in removing the obstacles completely. That is unimportant. What is important is the commitment to the struggle to overcome them.

Jesus told a parable about a king whose enemy was marching against him. The king counted his troops to see whether he had a chance of defeating the enemy. Only after he clearly knew his resources and had weighed his chances of winning could he decide whether it was better to march out to meet the enemy or to try to make peace before fighting.

We have to identify clearly the obstacles on our spiritual journey and the resources we have to meet them before we can decide whether to wrestle with them without giving an inch, to bend a bit, or to acknowledge that by ourselves we are powerless against them. The first step in our struggle is to come to grips with our limits.

The most significant obstacles on the spiritual journey come from within: weaknesses, bad habits, negative feelings and attitudes that we have formed and chosen over the years. We carry these obstacles to growth with us and often do not recognize them when they are at work.

Sometimes we live in the past and let unhealed wounds and disappointments color the present. Unhealed wounds can give rise to feelings of failure, guilt, bitterness, low self-esteem, and anger. These can create roadblocks to the openness required for healthy relationships. The struggle may well be to leave the past behind and accept the inner healing offered by Jesus. This inner healing also applies to physical problems. If we are sick, run down, overweight, or preoccupied about the condition of our health, we lack the energy needed to pursue the journey with zest and vigor. The healing may take the form of proper exercise, healthy meals, or proper rest. This may demand that we curtail some of the things we want to do or like to do.

- Each of the words and phrases listed below can be seen as a brick in a wall that blocks your spiritual journey. On the line before each word or phrase, rate the extent to which you feel it is a reality in your life, 0 being the least and 5 being the greatest.

  ___ past hurts
  ___ anger
  ___ guilt
  ___ bitterness
  ___ burnout
  ___ fear
  ___ boredom
  ___ stress

____ workaholism
____ too much sleep
____ too little sleep
____ poor diet
____ poor relationships
____ excessive recreation
____ anxiety
____ pessimism
____ rigidity
____ dwelling on the past
____ worry about the future
____ feeling insecure
____ feeling misunderstood
____ alcohol and other drugs

- Pick the two or three bricks you have marked highest and write a few sentences about how each brick affects your life.

Anxiety about the Future

Anxiety about the future can also prevent us from being open and taking necessary risks in the present. Excessive anxiety about the future can produce fear, despair, and pessimism, and create massive roadblocks on the spiritual journey. The struggle is to face these anxieties about the future and by recognizing their presence and power in our lives, work to remove them one by one. If we see that we are actually powerless over some of them, we may hear the invitation to turn our lives completely over to God.

- List the biggest fears, worries, and anxieties you have about the future.

- List these worries, fears, and anxieties again, dividing them into two columns under the headings: "Things I can do something about" and "Things I can do nothing about."

- For each of the items you can do something about, write a specific action you can take.

- For those you can do nothing about, write your own prayer giving these anxieties to God.

Negative and Irrational Ideas

Another common obstacle on the journey is negative, irrational ideas. Dr. Albert Ellis in *Reason and Emotion in Psychotherapy* points out some of these ideas and calls on people to replace them with more wholesome and positive ideas about reality. At the heart of many of these negative ideas is a feeling that people have little control over their own lives and the world they live in. Here is a list of some of these ideas:

1. For me to feel good about myself, I must be loved or at least approved by virtually every significant other person in my community.
2. I should be thoroughly competent, adequate, and achieving in all possible respects if I am to consider myself worthwhile.
3. Certain people are bad, wicked, or villainous, and they should be severely punished for their villainy.
4. It is easier to avoid than to face certain difficulties and responsibilities in life.
5. It is awful and catastrophic when things are not the way I would very much like them to be.
6. Human happiness is externally caused. I have little or no ability to control my sorrows and disturbances.

7. My past history is an all-important determiner of my present behavior. Something that has strongly affected my life will continue to affect it indefinitely.

8. I must perform well and be approved by significant others. If I do not, then it is awful. I cannot stand it and I am an awful person.

9. You must treat me fairly. When you don't, it is horrible and I cannot bear it.

10. Conditions must be the way I want them to be, or I cannot stand to live in such an awful world.

- Which of these ideas are influential in your life?

- How do they affect your relationship with God?

- How do they affect your work?

- Write positive statements countering the irrational ideas that are most influential in your life.

Discouragement and Enthusiasm

Two hidden pitfalls on the journey are discouragement and enthusiasm. Discouragement, the shadow side of a sensitive soul, comes from seeing one's failures, one's weaknesses, one's troubles and trials but not seeing a way out, a redemptive path beyond the immediate negativity. It comes from failing to realize what it means to be on a journey. We are on a journey, not at the end of the journey. This means that we progress on our way best when we take but one step at a time. It implies that we can try again, that we always have time to do better and to change. The fact that we have been called by God means that we can surrender our lives into God's hands with confidence. Even in the worst of circumstances, we have more going for us than against us, because "God and I are a majority in all situations." The fact that we

57

are called to make the journey with others offers us the strength and comfort of sharing with others who are struggling as we are. Prayer does not always seem to be an effective weapon against discouragement, but it does put us in touch with the power of God by which we can take a risk and try once again.

Excessive or inappropriate enthusiasm is rooted in the insensitivity of the soul. Enthusiasm for the things of God is obviously not a bad thing. It generates life and energy and leads people to do God's work in the world. But sometimes a person is so captivated by particular emotional religious experiences that the pain, the need, the longing for the fullness of redemption is forgotten. Enthusiasm then becomes an obstacle on the journey. The struggle is to maintain a balanced enthusiasm, one that celebrates the presence of God and at the same time is in touch with the elements of life that speak of God's absence and of a longing for the God still to come. Listening to the experience of others, both past and present, getting in touch with oneself, and acknowledging one's limitations are helpful in giving balance to one's enthusiasm.

Saint Paul knew the struggle that comes from making Jesus the center of life. He acknowledged his weaknesses and his limits. He confessed that he had the desire to do good but not the power. He admitted that he did not do the good he intended to do, and did the evil that he did not intend to do. He cried, "What a wretched man I am!" but he was not discouraged *(Romans 7:15-25)*. With enthusiasm he could proclaim that he was justified by faith. He was at peace with God because of Jesus. He wrote,

We even boast of our afflictions! We know that affliction makes for endurance, and endurance for tested virtue, and tested virtue for hope. And this hope will not leave us disappointed, because the love of God has been poured out in our hearts through the Holy Spirit who has been given to us.

Romans 5:3–5

- What things speak to you of God's presence and give you enthusiasm?

- What things speak to you of God's absence and discourage you?

- What do you do to balance these things?

Obstacles from the Outside

Not all of our struggle is with our inner self. The culture in which we live is constantly pointing in different directions and trying to tear up the road we want to follow. It puts up signs all along the way: "This is all there is! There ain't no more!" "Get it all now while you can!" "You have a right to comfort and prosperity!" We are so deeply rooted in our culture that we have a difficult time seeing the unspoken assumptions on which this culture rests. We take for granted a consumer society and a lifestyle based on the acquisition and pleasurable use of material things. The primary struggles with our lifestyle revolve around our use of money and time. Each day we face the challenge of how we are to use the resources we have. Very easily these can become the center of our attention and the goal of our lives, rather than the means by which we make a contribution to future generations and move to a fuller, more comprehensive, richer relationship with God and with one another.

The resources we have to help us in this struggle are the Scriptures, the teachings of the Church, and in a very special way the lives of the saints. In spite of all the pious writings which make the great Christians of the past seem anemic, they were strong people, people who stood against the prevailing culture of the day. Many of them by their lives and teachings took a stance against the materialism of the age, especially against the materialism which infected the Church. A careful reading of their lives helps us counteract the unspoken assumptions of our time that it is the rich who are blessed or that Christianity is too idealistic.

- Look at some advertisements in magazines. What are some of the underlying assumptions about the purpose of life, what gives meaning to life, what is important, what makes good human relationships?

- Where do you find conflicts with the values of Christ?

- Where do you feel these conflicts in your own life?

The Heart of the Struggle

The direction a person's struggle with these various obstacles takes is very important. Jesus' battle with the tempter in the desert clearly pointed out two possible directions for Jesus. One was a self-serving direction of living up to the people's ideal of what a messiah should be. The other was an other-serving direction of doing what God willed, meeting the needs of the people and dying in the process.

Is one's life going to be only self-seeking, that is, only inner-directed, self-centered, an effort to find those things that one feels will make a person a complete and happy human being? Or is it going to be outer-directed, responding to the call to place oneself completely at the disposal of God? This is the fundamental question.

Some people who have embarked on a committed life struggle to fit into a certain self-ideal. They have a picture of what a "holy person" should be. Every day they struggle against many obstacles to conform to that self-ideal. Their struggle is self-centered and usually unsuccessful. Others embarking on the same course see that the struggle against the interior and exterior obstacles is a stretching to respond and conform to the Loving Other into whose hands they have commended themselves. The struggle is other-centered, a struggle to be open to the call of the Spirit, however it comes.

Even though the journey is one of relationships, of reaching out to God and to other people, it does focus on a person's personal commitment and faith life and identity. This focus is necessary and good, as long as it does not become an introverted, private exercise.

The struggle is not against interiority or the development of a faith life. It is a struggle to keep our vision wide, to see beyond ourself and our own little world. It is a constant struggle not to retreat from the world, not to think that "doing my thing" is most important. It is the effort to be involved in the world, to stay connected to people, and to expand our vision to include more people. The hunger of others becomes our own hunger. Their poverty, their homelessness, their suffering from violence and oppression become our own suffering. Their inner turmoil, and especially their failure or their inability to set their feet on the road of the spiritual journey, becomes our own concern. Their happiness, their security, their well-being become as important as our own.

The struggle is part of the pilgrimage. It is against many and varied obstacles, but it must always lead us out of ourselves to a deeper loving relationship with others.

- To what extent are your prayers devoted to your own physical and spiritual needs?

- What are some signs in your life that your journey is outer-directed, a response to the call to place yourself at God's disposal?

Practice

1. At this point in your life, what are the greatest obstacles on your spiritual journey?

_____

_____

_____

2. You cannot attempt to remove all the obstacles in your path at the same time. Look over the list of obstacles in the first reflection questions of this chapter. Pick one that you think you may be able to do something about. Write down one thing you are going to do for a week. Be very specific. For the next seven days keep track of how well you have done in working with this obstacle.

7

THE DISCIPLINE OF THE JOURNEY

The goal of the spiritual journey is a deep and healthy relationship with God and neighbor. To achieve this goal a person has to give shape consciously to the pattern of his or her life and strive to live by that pattern in spite of many obstacles. These obstacles, both exterior and interior, will not be overcome without personal discipline.

This discipline is the deliberate decision to employ certain patterns of action. All significant relationships require both spontaneous expressions of love and deliberate planning by the persons involved. For example, two people who love each other will marry and organize their lives to spend a certain amount of their time together. They may have to work, they may have to be apart for periods of time, they may have children. But if the marriage is to survive and thrive, the couple requires a certain amount of time together, and this time has to be planned.

Throughout the history of Christianity, various practices or patterns of living have been recommended to people who have embarked on the spiritual journey. Jesus himself practiced and suggested prayer, fasting, and giving to the poor. Such learned practices, or disciplines, are intended to help people remember and reinforce the movements of God in their lives.

In most people's minds, the meaning of the word *discipline* is negative: punishment in response to misbehavior. However, in its root meaning, it has the much more positive connotation of being an avenue of learning.

Christian discipline is practiced attention to the management of our lives in light of the commitments we have made, especially the committed attachment to the Lord. We need to learn how to remember and enflesh that committed attachment, whether considering the simple routines of daily life or the more critical and dramatic decisions. Discipline gives rise to disciplines, the particular practices by which we pay attention to our commitments. They are means to an end on the spiritual journey. They are not ends in themselves, nor are they a measure of spiritual growth. Love is the only measure of that.

- What comes to mind when you hear or read the word *discipline?*

- What experiences have helped create your attitudes toward discipline?

- How can you come to think about discipline more positively?

Poverty

The Gospels indicate several forms of discipline fundamental for all Christians. Later theologians have gathered many of these under the categories of poverty, chastity, and obedience. Because men and women who embrace the religious life take these vows, those who are not in religious life tend to think that these vows are not an essential part of the spiritual journey.

The previous chapter discusses how the national American lifestyle is one of the greatest challenges Christians in this country face on the journey. Advertising constantly tells people to surround themselves with the newest and best of everything—salvation and happiness are only one more purchase away. Because of this emphasis on consumerism, material things can very easily and very subtly become the center of attention and the goal of life.

The discipline of poverty helps people come to terms with the "ideal lifestyle" presented by our culture. Christian poverty is the discipline by which believers express their values in the way they use their time and money. *Poverty,* like *discipline,* is a word with many negative connotations. People tend to think it means destitution, the lack of all material possessions and of all provisions for the future. Rather, poverty simply means that our resources of time and money are allotted in a planned pattern to enhance our relationship with God and neighbor. It is the only way not to absolutize one's wealth. Only poverty can keep us from making money and possessions a false god that dominates our vision of life, our feelings, and all our decisions.

A pattern of allocating one's resources so that one remembers the goodness and generosity of God was built into the Law of Moses. It is called tithing. Most of the Israelites were small farmers or small merchants. Giving 10 percent of their income to support the priests and the Temple was a hardship. Of course, it was not as great a burden on the rich. Jesus indicated this when he commended the widow who gave her tiny coins to the Temple (see Luke 21:1–4). The 10 percent is not nearly as important as a consistent pattern of giving time and money, especially to God's children who are in need. Through this regular giving of resources, we can move to a fuller and more comprehensive relationship with God and neighbor.

Another way of living the discipline of poverty is to adopt the simple lifestyle of the Gospel. The best example of a Christian who did this is Saint Francis of Assisi. He took the words of Jesus literally: "Take nothing for the journey, neither walking staff nor traveling bag; no bread, no money. No one is to have two coats. Stay at whatever house you enter and proceed from there" (Luke 9:3). God does not call everyone to this stark simplicity. But the Gospel and the lives of saints challenge a lifestyle that is complicated by an abundance of material possessions. These possessions can become a real obstacle to the spiritual journey if we begin to depend on our own resources rather than on God. Jesus said to "seek first God's rule over you, God's way of holiness" (Matthew 6:33). This means allowing God to reign in our lives and may well demand that we simplify our lifestyles in order to surrender more fully to God.

Before moving on to the next discipline, we should look at one more aspect of poverty—poverty of spirit. Poverty of spirit, or detachment, goes beyond a simple lifestyle. It means a complete revision of all values because we have found the pearl of great price, union with God, and all other treasures we may possess fade in comparison. We allow the Spirit to direct and transform our thoughts, desires, and actions, so that all our judgments are those of Christ himself. This is what Saint Paul means when he says we are to "have the mind of Christ." To be this deeply in touch with the dying and rising of Jesus takes hard work and practice. It demands that we develop a sense of detachment in all areas of life. Detachment is not indifference. People with poverty of spirit care deeply because their perspective is through the eyes of Christ. They do not need to own or control to be happy. They are truly free because they are not ruled by the tyranny of possessions and selfishness. God has become the source of their inner harmony and peace.

- If you were to take seriously the discipline of poverty, what changes would you have to make in your life?

- What are two ways you could simplify your lifestyle?

- How can you be successful and assertive in your everyday life and still practice poverty of spirit?

- Jesus said that his followers must be clever as snakes and innocent as doves. Use your knowledge and experience of advertising methods to plan an ad promoting the discipline of poverty.

Chastity

Talking about the discipline of chastity, which involves sex, is not popular today, but such an ideal has been constant in Christianity since the time of Jesus. It is something that all Christians are called to live.

The sexual drive is the greatest source of human creativity and energy. It causes people to be attracted and energized when others come near. It is a source of life-giving power not only for procreation but also for ordinary human relationships. It can bring great joy to a person's life, and it can be a source of great destruction. A Christian approach to sexuality inevitably involves a commitment to use one's sexual energy in a positive, loving, creative way.

In marriage, two people commit themselves for life to share physical love exclusively with each other. When they make this commitment, both embark on a road of learning how to love and live with another human being. They are called to show spontaneously their love, their joy, their worries, and their feelings. They are called to create a family pattern by which they do this sharing in a regular way. Paul in Ephesians 5:22–33 even compares marriage to the relationship between Christ and the Church.

To live this pattern requires learning to communicate, to share thoughts and feelings, and to forgive. In establishing this pattern with each other and children, the couple are remembering and imitating God's communication, sharing, and forgiveness brought to them by Jesus Christ.

For those who are single, chastity rests on the same sort of commitment. It is a respect, a care, and a love for others that seeks only their greatest good. It is a commitment to God and a renunciation of genital pleasure at the expense of another. Any sexual expression that treats another as just a body or a thing to be used to meet one's own sexual desires is destructive to the persons involved. Deciding how to live out this discipline in specific situations is not easy and demands a great deal of thought and dialogue.

Some people even make a vow of chastity, or celibacy, which involves being free to love all those who come into their lives and to leave them behind when other demands are made. It is a commitment to more than one person, but it is not a permanent, lifelong commitment to any one person.

Chastity means using the creative sexual energy that God has given to bring life to others. Negatively, sex when misused is a big obstacle on the spiritual journey. Positively, since sexuality is one of the main ways people express love, it is a significant part of the spiritual journey.

- Do you have trouble thinking of sexuality positively, as a gift of God?

- How has your sexuality deepened your understanding of close relationships?

- Has the discipline of chastity been helpful to you? How?

- Read Ephesians 5:22–33. How does this passage help your understanding of spirituality?

- How does the passage help your understanding of sexuality?

Obedience

Obedience is another discipline or avenue of learning that applies to all people in one way or another. Human beings have a basic drive to be in complete control of their own lives and at the same time to dominate others. A person who thinks that he or she must have complete control of his or her own life is likely to use other people as things and to be unable to enter a true personal relationship with others.

Obedience is, first, the effort we make to hear and obey the many promptings from God each day. It is an effort to trust in God and allow God to lead us. Obedience takes many forms. It may mean putting aside our own wishes to respond to the needs of another. It may mean continuing to listen and dialogue with another to see how God is calling. It may even mean simply remaining open and listening to what life is calling us to do or be. But Jesus made it perfectly clear that the spiritual journey consists of hearing his word and of following him by putting that word into practice. "Anyone who desires to come to me will hear my words and put them into practice" (Luke 6:47).

Being obedient means showing that servant love of Jesus, who came not to be served but to serve. It means reaching out to those in need, even when it is inconvenient or when they seem untrustworthy. It means helping others without asking whether they are worthy of our help. It means forgiving when we have been deeply hurt. It means trying to share the message of God's love whenever possible.

Second, obedience is the response to human authority. In every society, there are duly appointed leaders, and there are times when those leaders have the right to expect compliance with the laws and regulations made for the benefit of the group. There are times, too, when we are in a position of authority, and the consideration of the other people's needs and desires, which is the pattern of obedience, must guide our decisions.

- Draw a circle for each of the three persons closest to you. Write the name of each person under one of the circles. Close your eyes and picture their faces in great detail. Think of what they are going through, their joys, their pains, their desires. Try to identify each person's greatest need. Write that need in the appropriate circle.

- Write one sentence for each person about how you can help the person meet his or her greatest need.

- In which areas of your life do you feel that you are under authority? How does this make you feel?

- What are some laws or regulations that drive you crazy?

- In what areas of your life do you exercise authority over others?

- What are some of the difficulties you have in making decisions for or about others?

Helps for Personal Discipline

It is not easy to determine the individual patterns of discipline that each person needs in order to be poor, chaste, and obedient. What seems clear in theory is often difficult in practice. How far to go, when to bend, when to resist are all questions that have to be settled on a case-by-case basis, but those who have reflected on these decisions have two recommendations.

The first suggestion is that we gather experiences. It takes effort and a deliberate decision to gather experiences. We tend to live from day to day without bringing together what has happened in our lives, reflecting on an experience, and drawing conclusions. The deeper meaning of an experience does not automatically become clear. It is only by reflecting and by comparing this experience with our previous experiences and with the experiences of others that we become clear about the direction our journey is taking.

There are many ways to gather our experiences. Retreats and days of recollection should serve this purpose. But there are other ways of daily or periodically gathering experiences. Keeping a journal is one such effective way. Keeping a daily or weekly log of images and symbols that are particularly important or striking in our lives is another. Taking deliberate note of our feelings, checking the direction and expressions of our anger, joy, or sexuality is still another. Through this charting of feelings in a deliberate and patterned way, we can come to understand the different movements of the heart.

The second suggestion is to consult regularly with someone we trust to help us. We all need a clarifying dialogue with another to help us understand the movements of our journey, to see the obstacles, to suggest options and courses of action. A good term for this relationship is spiritual friendship.

Another, more traditional form of spiritual guidance is spiritual direction. It also involves the dialogue of two persons, centering, however, on one person's experience of life in God. So, the experience of spiritual direction is less mutual than spiritual friendship. But for many, the greater objectivity is helpful in clarifying matters of the spiritual life.

Whether the relationship is spiritual friendship or spiritual direction, there is no room for one person to lord it over the other. Both are seekers and companions on the journey.

Discipline is essential if we are not to run around in circles or get stuck in a rut in our spiritual journey. We have to deliberately choose patterns of action that will help us keep on the way to the goal we have set and accepted for ourselves.

- What have been your experiences, positive or negative, with a spiritual friend or with a spiritual director?

- What qualities would you look for in a spiritual friend or spiritual director?

- If you have not had a spiritual friend or spiritual director as you worked through this book, what can you do to find one now?

Practice

1. At this point on your journey, in what one way do you most need to develop the discipline of poverty, chastity, or obedience?

_____

_____

_____

2. To help you discover the individual patterns of discipline in your life, begin the practice of keeping a journal. Each day, write down not only the important events of the day but also your thoughts and feelings. As the chapter points out, by charting your ideas and reactions in a deliberate way, you can more easily see the direction your journey is taking.

    It is often helpful when keeping a journal to have a simple, personal outline to follow. In that way, you can make more effective use of your journal. Use the space below to create your personal outline.

8

DISCERNMENT

On the journey of the spiritual life, there are many roads a person can follow. Some of these are dead ends. Others go in circles, so that after much effort a person ends up where he or she started. But there is a road—perhaps several roads—on which progress is possible.

Discovering which road to travel is one of the basic tasks of the spiritual life. The spiritual journey is not merely a matter of understanding God better or of feeling deeply about God. It involves making choices among various options open to us. Some of these options will hinder us on the journey. Others will hasten us on the journey because they lead to greater freedom. When we choose to remove or overcome the obstacles that block the ability to love, when we choose the welfare and happiness of another over our own, we are freeing ourselves to love. In many ways, discernment—choosing the right road or roads—is like choosing a pair of hiking boots. One pair is too tight. Another does not look right. A third pair may fit well but be totally inadequate for a long walk. Finally, we find a pair that is comfortable and will hold up for a long hike.

Discernment is not an exotic process; it is relatively simple. From the Christian tradition, there are five helps we can use in the process of discerning what to choose. Earlier chapters in this book have also touched on these helps.

Patterns

The first of these helps is reflection about similar situations to see what choices one has made in the past. This reflection is necessary in order to identify the patterns one's decisions usually follow.

Each person's life follows certain patterns. It is not a series of unconnected events. It is held together by a string of common threads. Some of these are helpful and healthy; others are destructive. Some of these patterns have worked well; some have not. Discernment is the process of sifting through one's experiences to find the common threads that run through past and present. Discernment leads to an understanding of our motives, which usually are rather obscure. When used regularly, it can help us discover our fundamental motivation. When we clearly see what stirs us to action and what directs our choices, we become freer to choose a course of action that is loving rather than self-serving. Discernment is more than voiding the mistakes of the past. It is more than merely repeating the patterns that worked well in the past. It is a process of looking for different, healthier, more growth-producing courses of action and choosing the ones that help us grow in our relationship to God and to other people.

It is not enough to look at one or two similar experiences. One needs to look at a series of them and identify what is common among them. What is common usually is not obvious and often seems to be but a minor factor in the experiences. It may take many years of reflection to identify the hidden operation of a basic fear or the subtle presence of self-indulgence in a life that on the surface seems to be devoted to God and to serving other people.

Once a pattern of acting is clear, our freedom is enhanced. The subconscious power of these patterns is weakened, and we are freer to choose among the options open to us. Discernment makes the difference between following blind instinct or unthinking feelings and making responsible choices. The truth that Jesus said makes us free is in great part the truth about ourselves and about our deeper motives.

Frequently, people try to discern the will of God for themselves only when they are faced with an important decision. They look for a sign outside of themselves to point the direction they should take. But when the big decision comes up, it is more helpful to reflect on the patterns we have followed in the myriad small decisions of daily life. From these patterns, the fundamental direction our lives have been taking becomes clear. Then we can more easily decide, in light of the present circumstances and of foreseen consequences, which path to take.

- When have you become conscious of a pattern of behavior that has helped or hindered you in making a decision?

- Think back over your life, and select a relatively common situation that you have experienced repeatedly. What decision have you usually made in those situations? What factors influenced your decision? How did you feel afterward?

- What makes it difficult to identify patterns in your life?

The Gospel

A second help in the process of discernment is holding up one's options to the mirror of the Gospel. The Gospel is a trick mirror. It does not reflect what stands before it but what should be. It reflects a person, Jesus Christ. The image we see in the Gospel is that of a man who sought in all things to be in harmony with God. Discernment, therefore, is a decision made with the aid of an image not of our desires but of Jesus.

This image is so brilliant, so overpowering, that it blinds. It has to be refracted, like light through a prism, so that we can look at single facets of Jesus as we make our choices. The compassionate Jesus, the humble servant of all, the forgiving judge, the reconciler, the devoted Son of the Father, the Lord crucified by the reality of sin are all mirrors into which we look for help in discerning what we are to do.

In his Gospel, Mark illustrates how this mirroring is a help in the process of discernment. Jesus and the Apostles were returning to home base in Capernaum. They were strung out along the road in groups of two or three. Those in the rear, out of earshot of Jesus, were arguing about which of them was the most important. They were all putting forth good reasons for their importance. Each could bring up unique attributes he had—ways of acting, decisions he had made—

that would guarantee that he would be first in God's realm. When Jesus asked what they had been discussing, they were silent, because they suddenly realized that being important was not high on his list of priorities. In fact, it wasn't on his list at all. Then Jesus gave them a norm: "Whoever wishes to rank first must remain the last one of all and the servant of all" *(Mark 9:33–37)*. Perhaps the Apostles had not been conscious of their real motives for wanting to be first. Perhaps all the reasons they had advanced to bolster their claim to priority sounded praiseworthy. But they certainly had missed the point of Jesus' life; they had to go back and reflect on their patterns of thinking and acting.

- Saint Paul says, "Your attitude must be that of Christ" *(Philippians 2:5)*. What attitude of Jesus is most difficult for you?

- What attitude of Jesus seems to be reflected in your life?

- What keeps you from turning to the Gospels for help in making decisions?

The Church

A third help in discerning which choice to make in a difficult situation is the Church. Ever since the first believers wrestled with the questions "Who is Jesus?" and "What must we do to be saved?" the community has been reflecting on its experiences and identifying common threads, or patterns, that can guide a person. It has put up dead-end signs, detour signs, and warning signs along the way. It has posted other signs indicating safe routes to follow. These latter directions, as is evident in the three basic disciplines of poverty, chastity, and obedience, point to a narrow, difficult road. But it is a road that many have traveled and have found to be the right one.

Some people would feel very comfortable if the guidelines provided by the Church were as clear and concise as those in an automobile association trip book, which indicates not only the best road to take but the exact distances one has to travel and the interesting sights along the way. The Church's help usually is not that clear and definite. It is found in various writings and teachings but, most importantly, in the lives of men and women who are called saints or great Christians. For example, we look into the Gospel mirror and see a poor man, Jesus. Then we look through the life of the Church and see another poor man, Francis of Assisi, who owned absolutely nothing but the clothes on his back. But we also find a cardinal, Charles Borromeo, who controlled a large fortune. He carefully tended it for his family but used none of it for his personal benefit. When famine struck Milan, he sold the silver plate in the archbishop's household but did not deplete the family fortune. These two saints did not practice poverty in the same way, but they certainly help us when we have to discern how we are to use the material possessions we have.

The liturgy is another way the Church helps in the daily process of discerning among the choices we face. Through the liturgy, Christians are kept in touch with the fundamental reality of the Christian faith: "Christ has died; Christ is risen; Christ will come again." Through the Eucharist especially, Christians are in touch with the living Christ, who is their model. Homilies and prayers bring a vision of what Christians can be and of the road to follow.

- In discerning which way you should take, when have you found the teachings or the liturgy of the Church helpful?

- When have you found the example of a saint or a great Christian helpful?

- Has the example of a personal acquaintance or modern Christian ever been helpful to you in making a difficult decision?

- What keeps you from turning to the tradition of the Church for help in making decisions?

A Community of Disciples

A fourth help in the process of discernment is the community of disciples. We can get feedback from the people on the journey with us, especially from a spiritual guide or friend. If we have someone who cares for us, knows us and is honest with us, that person can give us feedback on the decision we are considering or on the course of action we have been following. If we have a friend who has had to make the same or a similar decision and is willing to share what worked and what didn't work, we are very fortunate. If our spiritual friend is learned, he or she can suggest various options that we may not have considered. What we do *not* need in making decisions is someone who tells us what we are supposed to do or not to do. It is not easy to trust another with our secrets. It is very easy to think that our problems and choices are unique, but when we do find a person or a small group with whom we can be honest, we find that our problems are both unique and common.

- Recall a time when you received honest feedback from someone. How did you feel at the time? Was it helpful? Did it change the way you did things?

- Recall a time when someone trusted you enough to share something of his or her inner self. How did you feel? How did the sharing affect your relationship? How did it affect your personal growth?

- What is your greatest fear in entrusting your deepest secrets to another?

Hope and Prayer

The final help is prayer and hope. We do not have to be long on the spiritual journey before we find that it is very unpredictable. It is not under our control. It can take a sudden sharp turn at any moment. Our most carefully thought-out decisions can go awry at a moment's notice. At times like this—as well as when we are trying to discern what we are to do—hope helps us realize that God has been in our lives all along. God has been faithful in the relationship, and God will continue to be faithful. This realization gives us hope for the moment of grace in every difficult decision.

Prayer, communication with God, is helpful not so much as we ask for guidance, but as we are quiet and listen for the Loved One. God knows our needs better than we do. God knows the consequences of all the options we have. But God seldom intrudes on our decision in an overt, noisy way. Usually, God's guidance comes through insight when we are quiet and recollected.

- In your life at present, where do you need hope? What role does hope play in your life?

- Saint Paul wrote, "We know that affliction makes for endurance, and endurance for tested virtue, and tested virtue for hope. This hope will not leave us disappointed, because the love of God has been poured out in our hearts through the Holy Spirit who has been given to us" *(Romans 5:3–6)*. How can these words help you face the future with hope?

- What are two or three signs in your own life that your hope in God is well founded?

Practice

1. At this point on your journey, in what area are you struggling to discern what you should do or be?

_____

_____

2. Recall a difficult decision you made, one you had to labor long and hard to make. On the lines below, briefly describe the impact on your decision of each of the five helps discussed in this chapter.

   a. Patterns

   _____

   _____

   b. The Gospel

   _____

   _____

   c. The Church

   _____

   _____

   d. A Community of Disciples

   _____

   _____

   e. Hope and Prayer

   _____

   _____

9

REVIEW AND EXAMINATION

Each person's journey toward God is unique. But the common element of every journey, if it is to succeed, is the need to review and examine one's life on a regular basis. At first, most people are very enthusiastic about the journey. They feel strong and energized by their desire for a more intense spiritual life. Then, as the way becomes obscure and obstacles block the path, their resolve weakens. They grow weary of living up to their initial commitment, or practicing new patterns of behavior. This weariness creates frustration and can eventually lead to giving up the journey entirely. But if people take the time to review and examine their lives regularly, they can discover ways of dealing with their weariness and find the strength they need to persevere.

This review and self-examination should not be limited to faultfinding. While it is important to identify the obstacles, overt or hidden, that block our path, it is just as important to realize how much we have changed and how far we have traveled. The basic question in our review should not be "Where have we failed?" but "How much have we loved?" By asking ourselves the right question, we can get a much better picture of just where we are on our journey. When our answers lead to the discovery of unconverted areas in our lives, we can humbly ask for God's healing grace and continue on living the great and mysterious gift God has given us.

Seeing how well we have done on the journey is also important because sometimes the temptation is not to abandon the journey in some act of apostasy, but rather to forget that we are on a journey. Old habits creep back in. Unconverted ways of thinking assert themselves. Destructive ways of handling feelings continue to influence our choices and decisions. We allow the journey and the graced moments of life to wither from lack of attention.

Jesus expressed this truth in a very dramatic way:

"When an unclean spirit has gone out of a person, it wanders through arid wastes searching for a resting-place; failing to find one, it says, 'I will go back to where I came from.' It then returns, to find the house swept and tidied. Next it goes out and returns with seven other spirits far worse than itself, who enter in and dwell there. The result is that the last state of the person is worse than the first."

Luke 11:24–26

Review and examination are the discipline we practice to keep the old, rejected spirits from taking up their residence in us once again. The discovery of the unconverted areas of our lives, of our sins, and of our weaknesses, coupled with the discovery of the goodness of God that has been operative in our lives, is a great help in discerning the path we are to follow, the decisions we are to make.

- What are some of the bad habits that God has helped you clean out of your house?

- What signs are there in your life of progress on your spiritual journey?

- What are your main difficulties in doing regular self-review?

What to Look For

The examination of conscience found in many of the traditional books of spirituality was rather sterile, a laundry list of sins one would check off to see in which way one had failed. Self-review and self-examination are a much richer way of looking into oneself. There are various ways people can do this.

One way is to review the basic principles suggested in this book. We are on a journey from a life of loneliness to communion with God and with other people. We look at not only what we have done but how we have thought and how we have felt in various situations. We look especially for incidents when our thoughts, feelings, and actions have shown an openness to God and others, so that we can function in a similar fashion in similar situations. We look at our journey to see whether it tends to be intrapersonal—wrapped up in our own thoughts, feelings, and actions—or whether it is interpersonal—going in the direction of improving our relationships with God and with others. We check how we have been in contact with God through Scriptures and through prayer, both one-to-one and many-to-one prayers. We reflect on our relationship to the Church and on the obstacles that hinder us. We look back at the important decisions we have made to see how we have used the helps available to us.

The spiritual masters have suggested that this review be done in some form on a daily basis and on a more detailed basis at least once a month. It can be done alone. We take some time each day to see how well we have done. Then, we take a day or part of a day each month to review and to pray. Our models for this review are Jesus and John the Baptizer. They, too, went into the desert to be alone with God.

If we have been keeping a journal, we use it in our review of life. We look for patterns. We note the positive steps we have taken and the graces that we have received. We reflect on what we might do the next time similar situations occur. In the journal, we will probably be able to spot both detours and strides along the narrow path we have chosen.

Finally, if we have been sharing our journey with a spiritual director or a spiritual friend, we may want to talk with him or her about what has been happening in our lives. It is easy to share the events, the worries, the successes we have experienced. It is more difficult to share how we see God operating in our lives and how we are in relationship to God and others. Sharing the basic patterns of our lives is always threatening. We are not sure how someone else will react or respond, but we need to trust and hope that the person will still accept us. This deep sharing can lead to honest and helpful feedback. A spiritual friend or director can often perceive patterns more clearly. He or she may see progress where we have seen a detour, or a detour where we have seen progress.

- How helpful have you found keeping a journal?

- How has your spiritual friend or director helped you to reflect more on your life?

- How have you grown in your skill in reflecting on your own life?

The Necessary Mind-set

This self-examination is not a criminal trial before an impartial but just judge. We recognize that all are sinners. In fact, the more we use the process, the more we will recognize how far we are off the mark, which is the best definition of sin. At the same time, we recognize that basically we are good, that God loves us, and that in some mysterious way Jesus has saved us from our sins. So, we approach the self-examination with the mind-set that the Spirit of Jesus is with us, not to condemn us, but to enlighten us, to encourage us, to strengthen us, to teach us, to help us, and to accompany us along the journey. We are reflecting with a friend rather than pleading our case before a judge.

This realization leads to a confession of sin with a resolve to get back on the direct path. It also leads to a song of praise for the many graced moments we have experienced on the journey.

- How can relating to Jesus as your best friend help you continue your journey?

- What would you like to do in order to initiate or improve your self-review and your self-examination?

Practice

1. At this point on your journey, in what direction would you like to move?

_____

_____

_____

_____

2. Progress on the spiritual journey demands close attention to reality. Every moment can be a time of revelation, a message from God. Paying attention to the present moment and reflecting on past experiences are the keys to movement on the journey. They help you see God's hand in your life and recognize God's vision of love for you.

   A good example of how this works can be found in Joshua 24:1–28. Before his death, Joshua called the Israelites together and recounted all that had happened in their flight from Egypt and their conquest of the Promised Land. He pointed out that God was always leading Israel, even in the dark and discouraging times in the desert. Every event that occurred raised questions and called for a decision to press on. When he had finished, Joshua challenged the people to make a new commitment to serve God: "Decide today whom you will serve!" The people responded, "We will serve the Lord, our God, and obey the Lord's voice."

   Today, you are facing the same challenge. How you answer depends on the call of God and your desire for a closer union with God. This book has tried to give you some basic principles to follow on your journey, but only you can answer the challenge—a challenge that invites you to see all the moments of your life as opportunities to grow in love.

   Use this present moment to reflect on God's guidance and care for you in the past. Begin writing an autobiography to see how past events have led you to this stage of your journey. The following outline will help you in writing the history of this journey.

a. Break down your life into chapters, or periods. Begin each chapter on a new page.

b. Reflect on your entire life, writing down the important events that occurred during each chapter. Note especially those events that signaled transitions—going to a new school, beginning a different job, entering religious life, getting married or divorced, having a child, becoming seriously ill, watching a loved one die, and the like.

c. Put the history aside for about a week. Then, go back and flesh out each chapter by describing how you felt about the events at the time and how you reacted.

d. After a brief rest, write down your present thoughts and feelings about each chapter in your life and what each chapter reveals to you about God's love and guidance.

You may find that parts of this process will dredge up painful memories. But you will also discover moments of peace and joy. It is only by putting the past in perspective that you can move forward on your journey toward God.

As a personal reminder of your commitment, write the challenge of Joshua on the last page of your autobiography. Below the challenge, write your personal response and a prayer for help on your journey.

If you wish, use the following pages of this book to write your spiritual history and personal response. As you write, remember the words of Saint Paul: "By the might of God's glory, you will be endowed with the strength needed to stand fast, even to endure joyfully whatever may come, giving thanks to the Father for having made you worthy to share the lot of the saints in light" (Colossians 1:11–12).

Journey of Faith